# Danny the Cl of the World

## Classroom Questions

A SCENE BY SCENE TEACHING GUIDE

## Amy Farrell

SCENE BY SCENE

ENNISKERRY, IRELAND

Scene by Scene
Enniskerry
Wicklow, Ireland.
www.scenebysceneguides.com

Danny the Champion of the World Classroom Questions by Amy Farrell.
ISBN 978-1-910949-54-2

# Contents

# Chapter One
# 'The Filling Station'

## Summary

The narrator's mother died when he was four months old. Since then, he has lived with his father in their old gipsy caravan behind their filling station.

The narrator's father lavished him with love and he was a happy, healthy child.

The filling station is small, with two pumps, a wooden shed for an office and a fine workshop for repairing cars.

They live in a real old gipsy wagon without electricity, and are very content there.

# Questions

1.  Why does the narrator live alone with his father?

2.  Where does the narrator live?

3.  What are your first impressions of the narrator's father?
    Explain your point of view.

4.  Describe the filling station.

5.  Describe the gipsy caravan where they live.
    Would you like to live in a real gipsy caravan like this?

6.  Why is there no electricity in the caravan?

7.  How do they get their light and heat?

8.  How does the narrator have a bath?
    Does this sound pleasant to you?

9.  What is a lavatory?
    Where is their lavatory?
    What do you think of this?

10. What makes thumping noises on the caravan roof
    sometimes?

11. Is the narrator happy, living in the caravan?

12. Do they sound like a happy family to you?

# Chapter Two
# 'The Big Friendly Giant'

## Summary

The narrator thinks that his father was the most exciting and marvellous father that any boy ever had.

His father smiles with his eyes, not his mouth, and is a wonderful story-teller, making up bedtime stories every night.

One story, that went on for at least fifty nights, was about The Big Friendly Giant and his magic powders.

Danny asks his father if he has ever seen The BFG. His father tells him that he has only seen him once.

# Questions

1.  What opinion does the narrator have of his father?

2.  What makes his father appear serious?

3.  The narrator calls his father a "marvellous story-teller".
    What makes him say this?
    What does this tell you about the speaker's father?

4.  Have you heard of The BFG before?
    Give details if you have.

5.  What does his father do, as he tells his stories?

6.  What different features of The BFG story make it sound
    magical?

7.  Describe The BFG.

8.  What does The BFG carry with him?

9.  What does The BFG do with his magic powders?

10. Danny asks his father if he has ever actually seen The Big
    Friendly Giant.
    What does this question tell you about Danny?
    What is his father's reply?
    What do you think of this answer?

11. If you were in charge of designing this book, what
    illustrations would you include for this chapter?

# Chapter Three
# 'Cars and Kites and Fire-balloons'

## Summary

Danny's father is a fine mechanic and loves engines. Danny grew up in the workshop, learning how to be a mechanic.

When Danny turns five, his father does not send him to school. Instead, he continues to train him to be a mechanic. By the age of seven he can take a small engine apart and put it back together again.

He then starts school in the nearest village. His father walks with him, there and back, each day.

Danny is never bored with his father for company. One windy Saturday they make and fly a kite together. On another evening, he makes Danny a fire-balloon that rises up into the night sky.

Danny's father makes many things for him, including a soapbox whizzer for his most recent birthday.

# Questions

1.  Is Danny's father a good mechanic?

2.  Danny says that it was inevitable that he would be a
    mechanic.
    What does "inevitable" mean?
    What makes him say this?

3.  When Danny turns five, what problem must they think
    about?

4.  What hopes does Danny's father have for his future?

5.  Why doesn't Danny go to school until he is seven?
    Would you like to have been seven before starting school?
    Give reasons for your answer.

6.  Danny's father walks him to and from school everyday.
    What does this tell you about him?

7.  Does Danny lead an exciting life?
    Why is he never bored?

8.  How do they make a kite?

9.  Does Danny enjoy flying the kite?

10. What does Danny's father use to make the fire-balloon?
    Have you ever heard of or come across fire-balloons
    before?
    If so, where?

11.      Where does Danny find the fire-balloon?

12.      What promise does Danny's father ask him to make about the fire-balloon?
Is this fair?

13.      What other things does Danny's father make for him?

14.      What did Danny's father make him for his last birthday?
Is this a good gift?
Does Danny like it?

15.      What does Danny say about his ninth year?
What is your reaction to this?

# Chapter Four
# 'My Father's Deep Dark Secret'

## Summary

Danny says that as you get older, you realise that grown-ups have secrets.

A secret of his father's leads them into the adventures of this book.

One night Danny wakes up and his father is not there, nor is he in the workshop. Danny goes outside and calls him, but gets no answer. He is afraid that his father has fallen and banged his head.

He takes the torch from the workshop and goes looking for him, but cannot find him. He sits on the platform outside the caravan with a blanket around his shoulders, and waits.

When his father returns, he tells Danny that he was in Hazell's Wood, poaching. He says poaching is an art, but Danny is shocked to learn that his father is a thief.

His father caught poaching fever when he was ten, poaching with his dad. Back then, many families poached pheasants as times were so hard.

His dad says poaching is an exciting and fabulous sport that you cannot give up once you start.

Danny's father makes them sandwiches while telling Danny about the rearing of pheasants by the rich for pheasant shooting.

His father says that the methods poachers use to catch pheasants are secret. Danny asks his father to tell him about them.

# Questions

1. According to Danny, what do you learn about parents as you get older?

2. What does Danny realise when he wakes up during the night?
   What does he do next?
   What would you do?

3. What does Danny think has happened to his father?

4. Where does Danny look for his father?

5. Where does Danny wait for his father?
   How is he feeling, as he waits?
   What is the atmosphere like at this point?

6. Where was Danny's father?

7. What is poaching?
   How does Danny react to hearing that this is what his father was doing?
   Do you understand his reaction?

8. What were times like when Danny's dad was growing up?

9. What is so attractive about poaching, according to Danny's father?

10. Why do the keepers have guns?

11.    What is "Poacher's bottom"?
       Is this a funny or disturbing story about Danny's Grandad,
       in your opinion?
       Explain your point of view.

12.    What is Danny's father's view of pheasant shooting?

13.    What do they have for their midnight feast?

14.    Does poaching sound exciting to you?

15.    Are you surprised by Danny's dad's secret?

# Chapter Five
# 'The Secret Methods'

## Summary

Danny's grandad studied poaching intensely, even keeping roosters to practise on.

Danny's father's first big secret about poaching is that pheasants love raisins. He tells Danny about *The Horse-hair Stopper*, a silent method of catching pheasants, and *The Sticky Hat*, which involves covering a pheasant's head with a paper hat so that it cannot see.

Although he did not catch any pheasants tonight, his dad still had a marvellous time.

This is the first time that he has gone poaching since his wife died, and he apologises to Danny for leaving him alone at home.

Danny says he will not mind if his father wants to go again, which makes his dad very excited.

He asks if his dad will take him along sometime, but his father makes no promises, saying he wants to get back in practice first.

# Questions

1.  What made Danny's grandad such a good poacher?

2.  What is the most important discovery in the history of poaching, according to Danny's father?

3.  Why is *The Horse-hair Stopper* such a brilliant method?
    Why is this important?

4.  How does *The Horse-hair Stopper* work?

5.  What does the Number Two poaching method involve?

6.  Did Danny's dad catch any pheasants on this occasion?

7.  Why does his father apologise to Danny?

8.  Why won't his dad take Danny along with him?
    Is this fair, do you think?

# Chapter Six
# 'Mr Victor Hazell'

## Summary

Danny's dad plans to go poaching in Hazell's Wood again. He does not like rich Victor Hazell, a wealthy brewer, and is happy to poach his pheasants.

Last year, Mr Hazell was rude to Danny when he came in for petrol. He threatened to give Danny a good hiding if he got dirty finger-marks on the paintwork of his Rolls-Royce.

Danny's dad told Mr Hazell that he did not like how he spoke to his son. He told him to pick on someone his own size the next time, and refused to serve him.

A series of inspectors called to their property after this, as Mr Hazell tried to run them off their land, but they never found anything out of order.

Danny and his dad spend poaching day working on Mr Pratchett's Austin Seven.

Danny's dad wants to arrive in the wood at twilight. He will be back home by half past ten.

Danny does not mind being left alone, but is worried that his dad could get shot. His father assures him that there are not as many keepers as in the past.

# Questions

1.  Why will Danny's dad always poach in Hazell's Wood?

2.  Describe Mr Victor Hazell.

3.  How did Mr Hazell speak to Danny last year?
    What is your response to the way he treated Danny?

4.  How did Danny's dad react to what Mr Hazell said to
    Danny?
    Was he right to behave this way, in your view?

5.  Who arrives the day after the incident with Mr Hazell?
    What is going on here?

6.  Why does another inspector turn up soon after that?

7.  What is Mr Hazell doing to Danny and his father?

8.  Do you appreciate why Danny's father enjoys poaching
    Mr Victor Hazell's pheasants?

9.  How do Danny and his dad spend poaching day?

10. Why does his dad want to be away by six o'clock?

11. Why is there no point waiting until it gets really dark?

12. What time will his dad be back by?

13. Why is Danny worried about his Dad?
    Is his dad worried, do you think?

14.  What is the mood like as Danny's dad heads off?
     Are you worried about him at all?

15.  How would you illustrate this chapter?

# Chapter Seven
# 'The Baby Austin'

## Summary

Danny tries to do his homework, but cannot keep his mind on his work. He imagines his dad arriving in the woods.

He goes to bed. He wakes up, alone, at ten past two. Danny is certain that something has happened to his father.

He decides to go after his dad, and has the idea of taking the Baby Austin. He has moved cars in the workshop, so knows how to drive. He does not think that he will meet any other cars and plans to go very slowly.

Danny is scared and excited as he drives on the road. He is worried about meeting traffic, as he is driving in the middle of the road. Also, he has to change gears, something he has not done before.

As he nears his turn for Hazell's Wood, a car approaches from the opposite direction. As they pass, Danny sees that it is a police car. He swings the Baby Austin through the gap he has been looking for. It bounces and fetches up behind the hedge. He turns off the lights. When the police car comes back looking for him, it passes him by.

They come back in his direction, driving fast, but pass him by again.

Danny slowly drives on towards the woods.

He takes the torch with him. It is very dark in the woods. When he calls his dad, there is no answer.

# Questions

1.    What does Danny do when his dad leaves?

2.    Explain Danny's father's choice of clothing for his poaching expedition.

3.    What do keepers do when watching for poachers?

4.    What time does Danny wake up at?
Why is he alarmed when he wakes up?

5.    What does Danny decide to do?
What would you do, in his position?

6.    What wild and marvellous idea comes to Danny?
Is this a good idea, in your opinion?
Explain what makes you say this.

7.    How does Danny know how to drive?

8.    Is Danny a good driver, do you think?

9.    How does Danny feel, as he starts to drive down the road?

10.    "Most of the really exciting things we do in our lives scare us to death."
Do you agree with the author here?
Give examples in your answer.

11.    What difficulties does Danny face when driving the car?

12.     How long will the journey take him?

13.     Why is Danny afraid that the motor will overheat?

14.     Why is Danny desperate to turn off the road as he nears Hazell's Wood?

15.     What makes Danny hide?
        How does he manage to hide the car?
        Is he lucky here, do you think?

16.     Are you surprised that the police are out at this hour?

17.     What is it like in the wood?

18.     How would you feel, in Danny's position?

19.     If you were the illustrator, what images would you include in this chapter?
        Give reasons for your answer.

# Chapter Eight
# 'The Pit'

## Summary

It is very lonely and silent in the wood. Danny uses his torch, despite the fact that the keepers could see its light. He shouts to his father, trying to find him.

As time goes on, Danny's voice trembles and he says silly things, feeling hopeless.

He hears the faint sound of his dad's voice and runs towards it. He discovers his dad in a pit. His ankle is broken.

The walls of the pit are twelve feet high. His dad must get out before morning, when the keepers will come for him. They have not recognised him yet, as he covered his face when they shone a light down on him, and he did not reply to anything they said.

Danny fetches a rope from the car. Using only his hands, his dad manages to climb out of the pit.

Leaning on Danny, he hops through the woods. His broken ankle is very painful and it is difficult to get back to the car.

Danny realises they have forgotten the rope, but his dad says that it does not matter.

Danny drives them home. His dad will call Doc Spencer in the morning. He will sleep on the workshop floor.

Danny stays with him and wakes up to the sound of the doctor's voice.

# Questions

1.    How does Danny feel in the wood?

2.    Why does Danny use the torch?
      Is this foolish or wise, in your view?

3.    How does Danny feel, as time goes on?

4.    Where is Danny's father?
      How has he been injured?

5.    Describe the pit.

6.    Why must his dad get out of the pit before morning?

7.    How did his father end up in the pit?

8.    Why didn't the keepers recognise him?

9.    Why does Danny go back to the car?

10.   How does his dad get out of the pit?

11.   Is his father badly hurt?
      Include examples in your answer.

12.   How do they get to the car?

13.   What do they forget to take with them?

14.   Why does Danny's dad ask him to go slowly?

15.    What vehicle do they pass on the way home?

16.    Where will Danny's dad spend the night?

17.    Was Danny's dad lucky to get away, do you think? What could have happened if Danny had not rescued him?

# Chapter Nine
# 'Doc Spencer'

## Summary

Doc Spencer looks at Danny's father's ankle and decides to get him to hospital right away.

Danny's dad tells the doctor he got injured in Hazell's Wood. He and the doctor chat about poaching pheasants and the doctor tells Danny how to tickle trout.

Doc Spencer is outraged when he hears about the pit that Danny's father fell into. He says he never liked Victor Hazell, and remembers him kicking his old dog once on the way into the surgery. The doctor used a blunt needle on him that time, to teach him a lesson.

Doc Spencer says Danny can stay with him while his father is in hospital, but Danny's father says he will be home that evening. He tells Danny to close up the filling station and go to bed.

# Questions

1. Why doesn't Doc Spencer retire?

2. Describe Doc Spencer.

3. Describe Danny's father's injury.
   What treatment will he need?

4. How does Danny react to learning that Doc Spencer was
   a poacher?
   What is your reaction?

5. Which method did Doc Spencer use for pheasants?
   Why doesn't it work?

6. How do you catch trout, without a rod and line, according
   to the doctor?
   Do you believe him?
   Have you heard of anything like this before?

7. How does Doc Spencer react when he hears about the pit
   that Danny's dad fell into?

8. What "filthy thing" did Doc Spencer see Victor Hazell do
   once?
   What do you think of this?

9. How did Doc Spencer teach Victor Hazell a lesson on this
   occasion?
   What do you think of this?

10.     What will Danny do while his father is in hospital?

# Chapter Ten
# 'The Great Shooting Party'

## Summary

Danny sleeps all day, waking at six thirty when the ambulance men return with his father.

Doc Spencer checks in on Danny's dad and gives Danny a pie that his wife has made for him, which Danny thoroughly enjoys.

His father is up at six the next morning, saying he feels great.

Things return to normal, although Danny notices that his dad broods a lot and is often silent.

One evening his dad tells him that seeing Victor Hazell drive past each night, sneering at him, makes him hopping mad.

He tells Danny that the shooting season for pheasants will begin on October 1st and Mr Hazell will stage a grand opening-day shooting party. Rich people will come from miles around for it because it is the best pheasant shoot in the South of England. Mr Hazell likes it because he enjoys feeling important.

Danny's dad wants to poach so many pheasants from Hazell's Wood that there won't be any left for the big opening-day shooting party.

His father is very excited as he imagines Mr Hazell's disappointment.

Danny thinks it would be impossible to get two hundred pheasants. His father agrees that the keepers make it difficult.

The keepers go home once the pheasants are safely roosting, but nobody has dicovered a way to poach a roosting pheasant.

# Questions

1. What does Danny do once the doctor drives away?

2. What wakes him up at six-thirty?

3. Why does Doc Spencer come to the caravan?
   What does this tell you about the doctor and his wife?

4. Describe Danny's father's cast.

5. Does Danny enjoy Mrs Spencer's pie?

6. How does his father feel the following morning?

7. Do his broken ankle and cast make life difficult for Danny's father?

8. What change has come over Danny's father?
   Can you think of a reason to explain this change in him?

9. What makes Danny's dad "hopping mad"?
   Do you understand why he feels like this?

10. What is significant about October 1st?
    How will Mr Hazell celebrate the occasion?

11. Why do wealthy and powerful people come from miles around on this occasion?

12. What is the cost of rearing a pheasant?
    What is your response to this?

13. Why is the pheasant shoot worth it to Mr Hazell?
    What does this tell you about him?

14. What does Danny's dad want to do?

15. Does this sound like a "fantastic marvellous thing" to you?

16. Why don't the keepers stay in the woods all night?

17. Do Danny and his father have a good relationship?
    Does Danny know his father well?
    Give reasons for your answer.

# Chapter Eleven
# 'The Sleeping Beauty'

## Summary

Danny asks his dad whether his sleeping pills would work on pheasants.
He suggests filling raisins with the powder from the pills, to use on the
pheasants. His father thinks it is a wonderful idea.

He imagines scattering the raisins and returning half an hour later to collect
the drugged birds.

He will bring Danny with him, as it was his idea.

They have fifty pills, which Danny's dad thinks will be enough for two
hundred pheasants.

Danny's dad comes up with a plan to be ready in time for the shooting party.
Danny will stay home from school on Friday and they will not open the
filling station, so that they will have time to prepare the raisins.

# Questions

1.   What idea does Danny have?

2.   What does his dad think of this plan?

3.   How, exactly, does his dad think this plan will work?

4.   Are you surprised that Danny is allowed to go too?
     What does this tell you about Danny's dad?

5.   Will fifty pills be enough?

6.   What will they call this method?
     Do you like this title?

7.   What plan do they devise to be ready in time for the
     shooting party?
     Have they thought of everything?

# Chapter Twelve
# 'Thursday and School'

## Summary

Danny picks an apple for himself and his father and they walk to his school together.

Danny's father has a vast knowledge of the countryside that he shares with his son on these morning walks.

Danny is quiet as he goes into school, mindful of his secret poaching expedition.

Danny's teacher, Captain Lancaster, is a horrid, violent man. All of the children are afraid of him.

The other teachers are nice, including Mr Snoddy, the headmaster, who is a secret gin drinker.

Even though he has lots of good friends, Danny never invites friends home. This is because he enjoys being alone with his father.

Danny and his friend Sidney get in trouble on Thursday morning. Captain

Lancaster accuses them of cheating when they whisper in class. Danny shouts back at Captain Lancaster that he is not a cheat.

Captain Lancaster uses his cane on Danny's and Sidney's left hands as punishment. The pain is excruciating.

When his father sees Danny's hand that evening and hears what happened, he is outraged. He wants to go and beat the daylights out of Captain Lancaster, but Danny stops him.

Instead of a story that night, Danny's dad tells him the plan for what they will do in Hazell's Wood. They are so excited that they cannot sleep, so have a midnight feast instead.

# Questions

1.     What does Danny do before school on Thursday?
   Do you agree that this is a "marvellous thing" to be able to do?

2.     Why does Danny love the morning walks to school?

3.     Does Danny's father know a lot about nature?

4.     What does Danny learn about weasels?
   Did you already know this?

5.     Why are grasshoppers lucky, according to Danny's father?

6.     Describe Danny's school.

7.     Describe Miss Birdseye and Mr Corrado.

8.     Describe Captain Lancaster, Danny's teacher.
   What would school be like, with a teacher like this?

9.     Describe Mr Snoddy, the headmaster.
   What secret does he have?

10.     What stops Danny and his friend Sidney Morgan from telling the other children about Mr Snoddy's secret?
    What does this tell you about Danny?

11.     What is Mrs Snoddy like?

12.     Why doesn't Danny invite his friends home?
        Are you surprised by this?

13.     Why does Danny get in trouble with Captain Lancaster
        on Thursday morning?

14.     What do you think of the way Captain Lancaster treats
        the boys?

15.     Why does Danny shout back at him?
        Do you understand why he does this?

16.     How does Captain Lancaster punish the boys?
        Is this punishment painful?
        What is your response to this?
        Do you think that it is right, that teachers could hit
        students in the past?

17.     How is Danny's hand afterwards?

18.     How does his father react when he hears what Captain
        Lancaster has done to his son?
        Do you think this is an appropriate reaction?

19.     Why does Danny stop his dad from going to Captain
        Lancaster's house?
        Is Danny right to stop his dad?

20.     Why is there no bedtime story that night?

21.     Why can't they sleep when they go to bed?
        What do they do instead?

22. What have you learned so far about the world of this story, the time and place it is set in?
    Is it very different from today?
    Include examples in your answer.
    Would you like to live in a place like this?
    Give reasons for your answer.

23. What is Danny like, based on everything you have read so far?
    Include examples in your answer.

24. What is Danny's father like, based on everything you have read so far?
    Include examples in your answer.

# Chapter Thirteen
# 'Friday'

## Summary

Danny feels excited and anxious from the moment he wakes up.

He and his father prepare the raisins in their caravan. His father talks about how good Danny's mother was at knitting and sewing. She used to go poaching with him too.

When they break for lunch, Danny cannot eat. His dad says he was the same before his first time poaching.

Just as they are getting ready to set off, a woman arrives looking for fuel. She remarks that Danny looks jumpy as he fills the tank.

# Questions

1.     How does Danny feel on Friday morning?

2.     How do they prepare the raisins?

3.     What does Danny learn about his mother as they prepare the raisins?

4.     Is this a sad moment in the story?
   Explain your point of view.

5.     Why can't Danny eat?
   Have you ever felt like this?

6.     Why must they leave the filling station at a quarter to six?

7.     Why does the woman think that Danny is going to the dentist?

8.     What sort of mood is his father in this evening?

9.     How would you feel, in their position?

# Chapter Fourteen
# 'Into the Wood'

## Summary

Danny and his dad get ready and head off along the road. They are excited about the night ahead.

Danny's dad tells him that pheasants, like all wild game, only belong to you when they are on your land.

They quietly make their way into the woods. They crawl the last bit towards the clearing where they see at least two hundred plump pheasants strutting about.

Danny's father spots a keeper over by a big tree. To start with, he throws raisins into the clearing one at a time, but when the keeper looks away, he throws in a whole handful.

The keeper steps forward, looking for them. Danny's dad is having a great time.

They wait for ages and then begin to crawl again, before running back out the way they came. Danny's dad is very happy with how it went and tells

Danny that he is proud of him.

# Questions

1.  What has Danny's dad tied around his belly?

2.  What sort of evening is it?

3.  How will they avoid the pit in the wood?

4.  According to Danny's dad, what is the fun of the whole thing?
    Would you like to do something like this?
    Give reasons for your answer.

5.  What interesting legal detail about pheasants does Danny's dad mention?
    Why is this significant?

6.  What is it like in the wood?

7.  Why are there always plenty of pheasants in the clearing?

8.  How do Danny and his father communicate without speaking in the woods?

9.  Describe the pheasants in the clearing.

10. Describe the keeper by the big tree.

11. What happens when Danny's dad throws a whole handful of raisins into the clearing?

12. Is Danny's dad having a good time? Why/why not?

13. Is Danny having a good time, do you think?

14. Does the first stage of their plan go well?

15. Do you think they will manage to pull this plan off successfully?

# Chapter Fifteen
# 'The Keeper'

## Summary

Danny and his dad sit on a grassy bank and wait for darkness to fall.

A keeper and his dog appear and walk down the track towards them. The keeper knows them and tells them to get going. Danny's dad replies that it is a public footpath, but when the keeper refers to his cast, they get going.

They slip into a nearby field and wait for the keeper, Mr Rabbetts, to leave.

Once he has passed, they return to the wood.

# Questions

1. What do Danny and his father do while they wait to return to the wood?

2. Describe the keeper that appears on the track.

3. How does Danny's dad speak to him?

4. Is Danny's dad worried about Mr Rabbetts, the head keeper?
   Explain your point of view.

5. Why do Danny and his dad hold their breath when the keeper passes?

6. Is this an exciting moment in the story? Why/why not?

# Chapter Sixteen
# 'The Champion of the World'

## Summary

Danny and his dad make their way through the wood to the clearing once again. As they wait, Danny's dad wonders if the pills will affect the birds and make them fall from their perches.

They hear a soft thump in the wood behind them and pheasants begin to fall to the ground. Danny's father is thrilled as they gather the fallen birds together.

Danny wants to leave, but his father insists on counting the pheasants first. He counts a hundred and twenty birds, a world record, and calls Danny the champion of the world for having the idea in the first place.

They fill two flour sacks with the pheasants and take the birds out of the woods to a waiting taxi.

# Questions

1. What is it like, in the wood?

2. What concern does Danny's dad have as they wait in the clearing?

3. What do they hear behind them?

4. How does Danny's father react when the pheasants fall?

5. What does Danny want to do when the pheasants are gathered?

6. Why does his father call him the champion of the world?

7. What state are the pheasants in?

8. How will they get the pheasants home?

9. How would you be feeling now, if you were Danny?

# Chapter Seventeen
# 'The Taxi'

## Summary

Danny's dad is full of pride and excitement as they make their get-away in Charlie Kinch's taxi.

Charlie laughs at the idea of the disappointed rich folk at the shooting party the next day.

Danny's father plans to share the pheasants amongst his friends, including, to Danny's surprise, the local policeman.

They drop the birds to Mrs Clipstone, the vicar's wife, in case a keeper is waiting for them at home.

Danny is shocked to learn of all the respectable local people involved in poaching.

They leave the birds in the vicarage's coalshed and begin to walk home.

# Questions

1.   What is the mood like in the taxi?

2.   Is Charlie Kinch, the taxi driver, impresssed with their haul?

3.   What will they do with the pheasants?

4.   Why must you always walk home empty-handed after a poaching trip?
     Is this clever of Danny's father?

5.   Why do they go to Mrs Clipstone's?

6.   Why is Danny continually shocked when his dad mentions local people who poach?

7.   Why does Danny's dad think that they have done the birds a kindness?
     Is there truth in what he says?

# Chapter Eighteen
# 'Home'

## Summary

Danny's dad is thrilled as they walk home in the moonlight together. He cannot believe that they have bagged one hundred and twenty prime pheasants from Victor Hazell's wood.

Danny's dad says they will need an electric oven and a deep freezer, for roasting and storing their pheasants.

They see no sign of Mr Rabbetts as they arrive home.

# Questions

1.  Why is Danny's father so happy?

2.  How will they cook the pheasants?

3.  How will they store the birds?

4.  How used Danny's mum and dad cook their pheasants before he was born?

5.  Is Mr Rabbetts waiting for them when they get home?

6.  Is Danny's father fun to be around?
    Include examples in your answer.

7.  Do you feel sorry for Victor Hazell at this point?
    Give reasons for your answer.

8.  Do you feel excited or relieved now that the poaching expedition is over?

# Chapter Nineteen
# 'Rockabye Baby'

## Summary

The next morning Danny's dad calls Doc Spencer and asks him over. The doctor is thrilled when he hears what they have done and congratulates Danny.

Mrs Clipstone approaches, delivering the pheasants beneath her baby in its pram. They notice that Mrs Clipstone is moving very fast and that the baby is screaming.

A pheasant flies up out of the pram, followed by others. Mrs Clipstone reaches the filling station and lifts her child. A cloud of pheasants fly out of the pram. The sleeping pills have worn off.

The pheasants do not fly away, but settle all over the filling station. Danny's father remains calm. He tells Mrs Clipstone to take her son into the caravan. Across the road, a line of cars form as people stop to get out and stare at the pheasants.

# Questions

1. How does Doc Spencer react when he hears what Danny and his father have done?

2. How does Mrs Clipstone deliver the pheasants?
   Is this clever, do you think?

3. How has she fit all of the pheasants into the pram?

4. What do they notice about Mrs Clipstone as she approaches?

5. Why does Danny's dad let out a cry of horror?
   How would you feel, in his position?

6. What happens when Mrs Clipstone lifts her baby out of the pram?

7. Are you surprised by this turn of events?

8. Why don't the pheasants fly far?

9. Where do they go?
   Is this a problem, do you think?

10. How does Danny's father react to this development?

11. How does Mrs Clipstone react?

12. What is happening across the road?

13.     Is this a tense moment in the story?
        Explain your viewpoint.

# Chapter Twenty
# 'Goodbye Mr Hazell'

## Summary

Mr Hazell's Rolls-Royce arrives at the filling station. Mr Hazell starts shouting the moment he gets out of his car.

Danny's father remains calm through this shouting. He then points out to Mr Hazell that the pheasants are on his land and so belong to him.

Danny's dad calls Mr Hazell a bloated old blue-faced baboon, which further angers Mr Hazell. He shouts at Danny's father, asking what he has done to the pheasants.

Sergeant Samways, the local policeman, arrives on the scene. Mr Hazell accuses Danny's father of enticing the pheasants onto his land.

Danny's father suggests that the birds flew onto the filling station to avoid being shot.

The sergeant suggests that they try to drive the birds back onto Mr Hazell's land. They shoo the birds, who fly onto Mr Hazell's car, scratching the paintwork and leaving droppings all over it, to Mr Hazell's great annoyance.

Sergeant Samways tells him to drive off quickly to escape the birds, and he does so, despite some large pheasants squawking and flapping in the seat behind him.

The other pheasants wake up properly and fly away, away from the direction of Hazell's Wood.

# Questions

1. Who arrives at the filling station?
   How does he react when he sees the birds?

2. How does Mr Hazell speak to Danny, his father and Doc Spencer?

3. How does Danny's father speak to Mr Hazell?
   What does he call him?
   What do you think of this?
   How does Mr Hazell respond to this?

4. Who else arrives at the filling station?

5. What accusation does Mr Hazell make?

6. What alternative does Danny's father offer?

7. What solution does the sergeant come up with?

8. What happens when they attempt to shoo the birds over the road?

9. What makes Mr Hazell leave in a hurry?

10. What happens when the pheasants wake up properly?

11. Are you happy with how things have turned out with the pheasants?

12.    Is this scene funny or tense or exciting?
Give reasons for your answer.

# Chapter Twenty-One
# 'Doc Spencer's Surprise'

## Summary

Sergeant Samways disperses the crowd of onlookers. He, the doctor, Danny and Danny's dad, chat about the pheasants. The sergeant congratulates Danny on his idea and Doc Spencer says he will go far.

Mrs Clipstone joins them from the caravan. She is very concerned about her baby and is sorry that the vicar will miss out on his dinner of roasted pheasant.

The doctor brings her to the workshop, where there are six pheasants laid out on the bench. The doctor found them in the pram, they were the greedy birds that swallowed a lot of the drugged raisins.

The doctor drives Mrs Clipstone home and the sergeant cycles towards the village.

# Questions

1.      What do the doctor and sergeant think of all the pheasants at the filling station?

2.      How does Sergeant Samways react when he hears how they caught the birds?

3.      How is Mrs Clipstone when she joins the others?

4.      What do they see laid out in the workshop?
Where have they come from?

5.      Why does Doc Spencer tell Danny's father not to be sad?
Is he right, do you think?

# Chapter Twenty-Two
# 'My Father'

## Summary

Danny and his dad go and sit on the platform outside the caravan. His dad suggests leaving the filling station closed and taking a holiday for the rest of the day.

They will go tickling trout, but first they will buy the electric oven.

Danny asks if they can invite Doc Spencer and his wife to share their roasted pheasant dinner and his dad thinks it is a great idea.

Danny looks forward to the day ahead, knowing that with his father, there is always something fun and exciting ahead.

He tells us that his father was the most marvellous and exciting father any boy ever had.

The last page has a message for readers, telling them to be sparky, not stodgy, when they are parents.

# Questions

1.      What does Danny's dad suggest they should do for the rest of the day?

2.      Where does his father suggest they go?
   What is Danny's response to this?

3.      Why do they decide to get an electric oven, even with the pheasants gone?

4.      Who does Danny want to invite to dinner?

5.      What will they need to get to host their dinner party?

6.      How will they spend the day?
   Does this sound good to you?

7.      What is Danny's parting message for us?
   How does this make you feel?

8.      There is a final message on the last page of all.
   Is this a good message, do you think?

9.      Do you like this ending?
   Give reasons for your answer.

# Further Questions

1.     Describe Danny's character, using examples from the text
       to support your ideas.

2.     Describe Danny's father's character, using examples from
       the text to support your ideas.

3.     Describe Mr Hazell's character, using examples from the
       text to support your ideas.

4.     Why do Danny and his father have such a good
       relationship?
       Include examples in your answer.

5.     What is the mood like as the story ends?
       Can you explain what makes it this way?

6.     What lesson does the author share with us in this novel?
       Is this a valuable lesson, do you think?

7.     Describe the time and place this story is set in (the world
       of the novel).
       What is appealing about this time and place?
       What is unappealing about it?
       Include examples in your answer.

8.     What would you change in this story to modernise it?

9. In this story, hundreds of pheasants are to be shot at a hunting party.
   What are your views on hunting?

10. What are the main themes/issues in this novel?
    Explain your choices, using examples from the text.

11. What do you like about this novel?
    Include examples in your answer.

12. What do you dislike about this novel?
    Include examples in your answer.

13. Who is your favourite character?
    What do you like and admire about them?

14. Which character do you dislike most?
    Explain what makes you dislike them.

15. What different elements of the story combine to make this novel exciting?

16. Do you like the ending?
    Does the ending complete the story?

17. Was there anything in the story that you would have liked to know more about?
    Explain your answer fully, including examples.

18. Would this story make a good film?
    What actors would you choose to play the key roles?
    Explain your choices.

19.      What was your favourite part of this story?
Why did this section appeal to you?

20.      Does this novel remind you of any other novels, films or television programmes?
Explain your choices.

21.      Would you recommend this novel to a friend?
Why/why not?

# CLASSROOM QUESTIONS GUIDES

Books of questions, designed to save teachers time and lead
to rewarding classroom experiences.

# www.SceneBySceneGuides.com

Lightning Source UK Ltd.
Milton Keynes UK
UKOW01f2046191017
311295UK00006B/305/P